Au Revoir:
GOODBYE UNTIL WE MEET AGAIN

ISBN 978-1-954095-37-3 (Paperback)
Au Revior: Goodbye Until We Meet Again
Copyright © 2021 by Alyssa Simone

Yorkshire Publishing
4613 E. 91st St,
Tulsa, OK 74137
www.YorkshirePublishing.com
918.394.2665

Printed in the USA

Au Revoir:

GOODBYE UNTIL WE MEET AGAIN

I never say goodbye. I say, *au revoir*. Goodbye is so final. *Au revoir* means I will see you again.

—Tao Porchon-Lynch

Alyssa Simone

TULSA

Contents

Acknowledgments ix

I ~~Want~~ Need You..2

The Worst Feeling...3

I'm Waiting..4

The Gap Between Us 5

Just Talk to Me..6

Butterflies..8

If I Could Catch the Falling Stars 9

The First Day We Spoke...10

Habitual...11

Nothing at All 12

Something More Than Strangers...13

One Problem..15

Brave 16

Two Different Worlds...17

More Than Just a Toy 18

All at Once...19

Rehearsals Can't Change How You Feel 20

Frozen 21

Can I Tell You a Secret? 23

My Goal 24

I Thought...26

Just Friends 27

Vulnerability..28

How Do You Make Someone Fall in Love with You?......................30

IRL 31

If Only 33

One Step at A Time..35

The Aftermath 37

Flipped...38

A Little Something Known as Love 40

Too Perfect...42

Something About You 44

So Many Places 46

I Like You (It's Only Three Words)...48

What I Said...50

My Secret...52

The Best Day of My Life...53

Who Knew Fireworks Could Be So Bright?..55

A Messy Kind of Perfect..56

Swing Sets & Starry Skies...57

Blue...59

If We Never Met 60

A Love Too Good to Hide...61

Insane..63

The Stars of Our Hearts...64

My Best Poetry...65

I Can't Remember 66

The Five Most Dangerous Words I've Ever Heard 67

The Five Most Beautiful Words I've Ever Heard...68

Just A Few Months Ago...69

You..70

Without You 71

Sunset Soliloquies..72

The Chances We Didn't Take 73

The Sound of Your Voice...74

Always on My Mind...75

When You Hold My Hand...76

Why Do You Always Write About Love? 77

You Are Good, Too..78

One More Time 79

The Best Friend I've Ever Had..80

I Promise I Can Be That Someone 81

A Reason to Care..82

I Love You 83

Sappy Piece of Shit...84

Forever 85

Energy..86

I Refuse 87

We Need to Talk 88

One More Day...89

What You Said 91

Nobody Cares About the Broken...93

Empty 95
Tough Girls Don't Cry 97
Fragile 99
I Deserved a Better Goodbye..101
I Hate Love You 102
Too Perfect 103
Sweet Lies...104
For Just a Moment 105
Sleepless Nights..106
Why I Can't Write About You Anymore 109
I Miss You 110
He Doesn't Want You 112
Nostalgia 114
I Remember a Time..116
If You Were Here..117
The Colors of Us..118
I Remember the Person You Used to Be 119
Running Back 120
Remember? 121
Her 123
Jealousy 125
Is It Possible for Colors to Drain? 127
The Way I Loved You..130
Fading Away..132
Sometimes...133
Your Eyes...134
Cut My Hair 136
And Yet I Smile 138
My Heart Bleeds to Remind Me I'm Alive......................................140
You Don't Feel Like Home Anymore...142
I Tried to Fix You 143
Bad Poetry..144
Your Name..146
My Favorite Lie 147
Where It All Went Wrong 149
Memories No More...150
Can You Hear
My Heartbeat?..151
Over You...152
Only One of Us Was Hurting 153

The Idea of a Love...154
Truthfully Okay 156
I'm Happy You're Happy..157
A Love Letter to Myself...158
Lost and Found..160
A List of Love..161
I Wanna Use My Voice...162
Au Revoir (Goodbye Until We Meet Again) 164

Acknowledgments

I never would have thought that at the age of sixteen I'd be sitting down to write the acknowledgments page of my first ever published book. It's the kind of thing I would have fantasized about as a little girl, who spent her free time writing incoherent stories in one of the twenty six journals she kept stored in her desk, the perfect home for her most prized possessions. But this isn't just a daydream that my idealist mind decided to construct from scratch. Although it's still surreal, this is reality, and I am so incredibly grateful to have the chance to share my words with the world.

That being said, this could not have been possible without all of the undying support I received along the way. Ever since this poetry collection was nothing more than an untitled Google Document I created at one in the morning, I've been lucky enough to have the most encouraging publishing team, family, teachers, and friends I could have ever asked for. They believed in me even when I didn't believe in myself, and without them, I am almost positive I would have given up and allowed my relentless fear of failure to consume me.

First, I would like to thank the entire team at Yorkshire Publishing for seeing potential in my writing and providing me with this opportunity to finally get my book out there. From editing my whole manuscript, to designing a beautiful cover, to answering every single one of my questions, your staff has made this process smoother than I ever could have anticipated, and working with all of you has truly been an unforgettable experience.

Next, I must acknowledge my family. Mom and Dad, I know it would've been easy to push for me to become a doctor, lawyer, or basically anything besides a writer, but the two of you always urged me to pursue my passions. You taught me to never settle and reminded me how proud you were of all my accomplishments whenever I began to self-doubt. Jules, you have lifted me up every time I was down and I am so thankful to have a younger sister as wise as you. I'm glad to see you're starting to enjoy writing as much as I do, and I hope your Wattpad career takes off soon. I love you guys.

I would also like to mention Michele Wallach, my extraordinary sixth and eighth grade creative writing teacher. You were the one who made me absolutely sure that I wanted to dedicate the rest of my life to poetry, as your class was always the highlight of my day. It allowed me to unleash my creativity in a way no other course did, and your pure enthusiasm toward writing was contagious. Thank you for playing such an important role in my journey to where I am now.

I could write more pages than there are in this book about how amazing my friends are, but I will try to be as concise as possible. Youssef Refaat, thank you for having such an emotional, pained reaction when I showed you that poem from my Notes app during one of our hangouts. I know that sounds sadistic, but it convinced me that my poetry actually could resonate with other people and tug on their heartstrings a bit. Kerri Brophy, Lisa Daccache, and Laura Schroeder, thank you for eagerly telling your entire families I had been offered a publishing contract before I had even told my own and for making me smile on all the days when my heart was hurting a little extra. Laura Fan, Nancy Ling, Vanessa Tam, and Kristen Wang, thank you for hyping me up every step of the way and for working so hard to perfect your pronunciation of my book title. Daniel Briskman, thank you for being so willing to answer all of my grammar questions; I know how much you love showing off your knowledge. Mina Mitsopoulos, Sukaina Shivji, and Bryan Wang, thank you for being three of the most uplifting, kindhearted individuals in my life. I wouldn't want to imagine a world without any of you in it.

Thank you to everyone else who has stood by my side and made me the person I am today: Charley Baluja, Nicole Cavalieri, Eric Cholico, Marawan Elrashidy, Winnie Li, Angie Mohamed, Argi Monioudis, Charlotte Seid, Elizabeth Shvarts, Abigail Tenenbaum, Alice Wei, Daniela Yevdaev, and Michelle Zhang. And of course, I cannot forget about all of my other readers. The fact that you chose to take the time to read my book, of all the hundreds of millions that are in existence, really touches me. I hope you are able to find some comfort and familiarity in my words and that you learn self-love prevails above all else. Life is much too exquisite and grand to waste precious time worrying about the faults other people may find in you.

And finally, to every boy who has shattered my heart and made me feel like I was unworthy of love, as well as those of you who doubted me and told me I was nowhere close to reaching my aspirations, this book is proof that you guys were wrong about me. So thank you, because without all of you, I never would have learned to love and believe in myself the way I do now.

—Alyssa Simone

IMPORTANT NOTE

I don't know what's going to happen to this book.
(I also know this is a weird way to start off a poem, but
writing is supposed to be a bit messy, anyway).
Right now, I'm only a sixteen-year-old girl typing
away all of my wounds until they appear in the
form of poetry on my computer screen.
I also don't know if these poems will make sense
to anyone else but me, and that's okay.
But if you're reading this, I'm opening up my soul to you.
And if a part of your core tells you,
"I feel like this is about me,"
Just know that
It probably is.

I ~~Want~~ Need You

I want you.
I want you more than the sun wants to light up the universe.
I want you.
I want you more than the moon wants
to illuminate the charcoal sky.
I want you.
I want you more than these poems want to go on and on and on.
I want you.
I want you more than I want myself.
I want you.
I want you more than it is possible to want someone.
And that is why I will never give up on you.
Correction: I need you.

The Worst Feeling

The worst feeling in the world
Is wanting to talk to someone
More than words could possibly express,
But you don't know if they feel the same,
So you decide to play it safe
And you never talk at all.

I'm Waiting

When I'm looking into your ocean-blue eyes,
And you look back, my spirits instantly rise.
Envy takes over when you're gazing at her,
Time seems to become an emerald-green blur.
Butterflies swarm my stomach when you walk in,
All I want to do is hold your tinted skin.
I dare to believe that it's all meant to be,
But you have my heart and I'm missing the key.
I'm waiting for the day when you'll be all mine,
And if I'm in your arms, life will be just fine.

The Gap Between Us

You look so perfect
Standing over there,
But I am
Standing over here,
And the gap between us
Is screaming.

Just Talk to Me

Lately,

I've been missing

The sound of voices dancing in the air

And I crave something

A little more than silence.

So please.

Just talk to me.

I know the messy clumps of hair

That hang in front of my face

May not seem very inviting,

But I'm begging you,

Just talk to me.

I know that I might just be the quiet girl

Who tries to keep her eyes hidden,

But it doesn't mean I'm not

Dying to be with you.

I don't even care what

What we talk about,

As long as I get to hear

The sweet sound of your voice.

Just talk to me.

I know there are many of parts of me

That don't quite seem very pretty,

But I promise that if you dig
A little deeper,
You can find something truly special.
Please.
Just talk to me.
Before the words I've
Always wanted to say
Are choked back down.
Before it's too late.
Too late to tell you
How badly
I've wanted to talk to you.
All this time.

Butterflies

From the moment I first met you,

I knew you'd have the power to easily

Transform my caterpillars into butterflies.

The innocent creatures

With pastel wings and meticulous patterns

Always flock into my heart

When I see your face.

No matter how much I've tried

Telling them to migrate to safety

And save me from the pain,

Their hunger for something they cannot have

Remains far too strong.

On lonely nights,

I'm always unsure of how much longer

They can live like this,

But whenever you walk into a room

I am proven wrong,

And the butterflies become

More beautiful than ever before.

If I Could Catch the Falling Stars

If I could catch the falling stars
Without hopes and dreams slipping through my fingers,
I'd send my soul to the moon
Where its silver silhouette could explode
And light could live off of lullabies.
If black holes were invisible
And my thoughts could travel faster than light,
I'd soar and surpass the shadows,
Leaving behind a transparent trail
With glitter glinting through.
If all the galaxies in the world
Could fit within my palms,
I'd stretch seconds into infinity
Until its fluorescent fibers came into view
And its roots reached the impossible.
And if I could stay alive after
Stepping foot on the sun,
Trust me—I'd give up everything
Just to scorch my bones with
The sparkling celestial power
Of possibility.

Alyssa Simone

The First Day We Spoke

I still remember
The first day we spoke.
It was as if every doubt I'd ever had
Evacuated my body
And allowed ease to pour in
From every direction.
It was as if
Everything was going to be
Okay again
And all of that wasted time
I spent being scared
Didn't matter anymore.
Because on the first day we spoke,
I finally believed in something,
In someone,
In us.

Habitual

Talking became habitual for us.
I'd gathered the courage
To ask you about your day
Or what the geometry homework was
Or if you had any plans after school.
Even though my nerves
Sent off a thousand signals to my brain
That this was a bad idea,
I ignored them
And somehow
I never regretted it.
We were starting to become friends
And every time we talked,
We became closer and closer
To becoming something more.

Nothing at All

You have the power
To make my world complete
Just by talking to me,
But you also have the power
To tear it apart
By saying nothing at all.

Something More Than Strangers

If I'm being honest with you,
I don't know what we are.
Over time,
We've learned more about each other
And exchanged phone numbers
So that we could continue learning
Even when we were apart.
I like having a label on things.
I hate the uneasiness of not knowing
Where something is headed
And if any of it is going to
Be worth it in the end.
I know you could break my heart.
But I also know that
You've made me the happiest
I've been in a while,
So I'm not gonna give up just yet.
And for the sake of
Labeling things,

I'm going to give one to us.
I don't know how accurate it is
But it feels right to me,
So I guess right now we're
Something more than strangers.

One Problem

There is one problem

With our progress, though.

Ever since we

Started texting,

We've relied on that

To nurture our relationship.

It's become so much harder

To talk in real life

Because we don't have that beat

To think of what to say next,

We don't have

The letters aligned perfectly

At the tips of our fingers,

We don't have

A second chance

In case we mess up.

And this is what

Is so terribly wrong

With our society.

Brave

"Can I tell you a secret?"
You once asked me.
I read the message
In your voice
And it sounded like the wind
On a beautiful summer night.
"I think you're really brave,"
You finished,
And just like that
My whole world
Seemed to come alive again.

Two Different Worlds

Sometimes,
I almost forget
That the perfect
Human being
I see every day,
Walking through
The crowded halls,
Is the same person
I am lucky enough
To text until dawn
Breaks outside
My window.
They're the same person
But sometimes it feels
Like they're living
In two different worlds
And I wish I could figure out
How to exist in both
At the same time.

More Than Just a Toy

I pray that
You're not
Leading me on
Right now.
Whenever I think
We might actually talk
About our feelings,
We never follow through.
I need to know
What you see
When you look at me.
I need to know
If I'm more than
Just a toy to you.

All at Once

Just hit me already.
All at once.
I can't take the
False hope
And mixed signals
For another fucking day.
Just bash my
Heart into a billion pieces.
The truth hurts
And so
The truth shall be told.

Rehearsals Can't Change How You Feel

Every night,
I rehearse saying your name
In a way that
Can make you fall in love with it.
I always think I've got it down
Until we're in the moment
And my pounding heart
Takes over.
But I know
You don't feel anything special
From the way I say your name.
I know
You don't feel anything special
From me.

Frozen

As much as I want
To let my feelings
Pour out of my heart,
The words are frozen
In my throat.
I count as the opportunities
Pass me by
Again and again,
Desperately trying to reach out
And grasp any lingering chances,
But my whole body
Is frozen.
There are so many things
I want to say to you,
So much love
I want to give to you,
But my thoughts
Always stop in their tracks,
Leaving regret to consume me.

I like you.
A lot.
But you will never know this
Because my words—
They're frozen.

Can I Tell You a Secret?

Can I tell you a secret?
The truth is that
Even if you text someone
Every single day,
And wave to each other in real life
During those fleeting moments when
You feel extra brave,
You're never
Going to get anywhere
Until you actually
Swallow your fears
And start speaking
To each other
In person.

My Goal

During one of our deep conversations,
You told me that you don't really care
Too much or too little about anything.
You don't feel too much happiness
Or too much sadness
Despite the circumstances.
But my goal throughout this journey
Is to teach you to stop being afraid
Of feeling.
I want to make you vulnerable
In the best possible way,
I want to set your soul on fire
So we can both burn down forests
With pure euphoria,
I want to get drunk with you
On simply being alive,
I want to tell you
To stop living life so blandly,
On a scale of zero to one hundred,
Because the truth is that
You are one in seven billion,
And there is nothing more
Astonishing than that,

And, no matter what happens in the end,

If I can make you feel

The entire world

Rushing through your fingertips

For just a fraction of a moment,

Then I will have absolutely no regrets

Because it means that I was able to save you

From yourself

Before it became too late.

Alyssa Simone

I Thought

I thought things
Were going great.
I might have even thought
That I had a shot
Until I see you with her
Laughing in the halls,
Looking at her
As if she's everything
You've ever wanted,
Your faces lighting up
When you see each other
And I can't help but wonder
Where she came from,
Why I'm not good enough,
And, most importantly,
What the hell
I'm doing wrong.

Just Friends

My friends can see the pain
Engulfing my entire day,
So they try to get the facts.
My stomach churns,
Digesting my organs,
Making me want to throw up
Every hope and dream I've ever had.
By the end of the day,
One of my closest friends
Comes running over to me,
And says with a smile,
"You've been worrying for nothing!
They're just friends!
Nothing more than that!"
I should feel better by this,
But I saw the way you looked at her,
And something about "just friends"
Just doesn't seem
Convincing enough.

Vulnerability

I keep telling myself
That it's okay
To take things slowly,
To steady myself
Before falling too hard,
To breathe for a second
Before allowing my feelings
To swallow me whole.
But how much time
Is too much time?
It feels like it's been forever
And I still can't bring myself
To look into your beckoning eyes,
To smile when you enter a room,
To actually talk to you
Without staring at a screen
The entire time.
I'm more scared than
I've ever been before
Because I don't want
To grow apart,
I don't want to lose
Whatever it is that we have.

For the first time in my life,
I am completely vulnerable,
And if I'm being real,
You're the best thing that
Has ever happened to me,
And I don't think I could stand
To lose that again.

How Do You Make Someone Fall in Love with You?

How do you
Make someone
Fall in love with you?
According to everyone
I've asked,
All the websites
I've searched,
And the deepest chambers
Of my heart,
You can't,
And it's the most
Soul-crushing
Realization
I think I've ever had.

IRL

Opportunities
For talking in real life
Hardly ever even come our way.
How is it that
I always manage to screw them up
When they do?
We were crossing paths
And all I had to do
Was summon the courage
To wave.
Just a stupid wave.
How hard
Could that possibly be?
However,
Your gaze stayed
Fixed ahead of you,
Seemingly staring at something
That wasn't even there,
As I desperately tried
To catch your eye,
Waiting for a signal,
An acknowledgment,
Something that

Made it okay to talk.
But I never received anything
And this is what happens
Every single time,
The unfortunate truth behind
Why you and I,
Clearly so perfect for each other,
Cannot seem to figure out how
To talk
In real life again.

If Only

Just when doubt
Is beginning to creep
Back into my mind,
You text me and say,
"If only we talked
In real life again."
I am taken aback,
Reading your words,
Over and over,
Wondering why they sound
Like a wish upon a star.
But that one text
Turned my whole world around.
That one text
Ignited a spark somewhere
From deep within,
Begging me to
Keep on trying.
I'm tired of sitting around,
Doing nothing,
And expecting my life to change.

I am going to
Talk to you again,
Whether we're
Ready for it
Or not.

One Step at A Time

When I wake up,
I decide that
Today is the day
Where I make a change.
I welcome bravery
To enter my being
With open arms,
My heart fluttering,
My thoughts blurring.
Keeping a positive mindset,
And dressing myself
With confidence,
I walk straight up to you
And say "Hi."
From there,
We keep on going
And it feels just like
Old times.
It feels just right.
At the end of the day,
I shower in pride
Because step one
Is now complete.

We got this.
We're gonna make it
One step
At a time.

The Aftermath

Ever since then,
We've been talking in person
Every day,
Without skipping a beat.
And every time,
I fall for you
Over and over
Again.

Flipped

Everything is flipped now.
I used to initiate
All our conversations,
But now
You text first
Almost all the time
And we practically talk
Every day.
It doesn't feel forced
And I don't need to
Wrack my brain
About what to say next.
Instead,
It comes naturally.
Everything has just been
So much better
Since we started speaking
In real life.
It's almost as if
You want to be
Talking to me.
But why me?
What makes me any better

Than that girl
In your English class,
Or the one you're always
Joking around with,
Or the one I saw you
Walking to school with?
Maybe I'm not any better.
Maybe you're talking to them
Even more than
You're talking to me.
But I guess
I'll never know.
So for now,
I just hope
That we don't find a way to
Flip back.

A Little Something Known as Love

Today I decide to
Do something
That lies a bit beyond
The boundaries
Of my comfort zone,
And send you
A cute little text.
"Hey,
I just wanted to let you know
That you're a great person
And I really hope
You know that."
When your reply comes in,
I read it over,
Again and again,
Not believing the words.
"So are you.
My life has
Improved significantly
Since meeting you."
My eyes fill with tears.
Happy tears.

The fact that I was able to
Make the life of someone
As incredible as you
Even better
Is almost too much
To handle.
Wow.
I did that.
And then I realize
That you had the
Exact same effect
On my own life.
And I think
This is a little something
Known as love.

Too Perfect

You're almost too perfect
To be real.
You have a heart
Made out of pure gold.
I saw you give up
Your seat on the bus
For an elderly man
As he walked on
And you thought no one noticed,
But his smile was bubbling over
With gratitude
And it spread to
Everyone around you.
You're so intelligent
And it blows my mind
Every single day
When you always have the answers
To the most difficult questions,
Never failing
To impress me.
You're probably the funniest
Person on the planet.
The jokes you make

Could keep me laughing
Until my cheeks become sore
And my heart
Aches with joy.
You're absolutely adorable,
With the most
Contagious smile
The world has ever seen
And the most radiant eyes
Even on the darkest of days.
There's no denying it.
You are utterly,
Completely,
And indisputably
Perfect.
I just wish you could
Say the same about me.

Something About You

There's just something about you.
I know I shouldn't want it,
But I need you.
Because, even though I know we won't work,
There's something about you.
Something about the way wrinkles engulf your blue eyes when
You smile,
And every single time,
I'm pretty sure the universe
Forgets how to breathe for a while.
Something about the way our eyes lock
From across the room,
But we nonchalantly look away
For neither one of us has the courage
To find happiness.
Something about the way you act so chill
And tell me that grades are just numbers
When I'm stressing out over them,
And how, each time,
I manage to feel so much better afterward.
Something about the way you blast the song you know annoys me
And belt out the words with a passion.
Something about the way you address me by my name

Because it just sounds so much better
In the tone of your voice.
It makes my heart pound relentlessly
And you always come up with the stupidest things to say,
Yet I appreciate it just the same,
For anything that comes from you
Holds inexplicable meaning.
I have no idea what it is,
But there's something about you
That I can't live without.
Something about the way we're so open with each other
Because you know that the boy on the
football team shattered my heart,
And you try so hard to mend it every single day.
I ramble off a list of traits I look for in a guy
As you diligently type them into your notes
But, in reality, there's nothing more I could ever ask for
Than that something about you.

So Many Places

You've touched me in so many places
That it's making me lose my mind.
You've touched me with your words,
Dipped in honey and trickling through my bones,
Sweet words that I savor in my heart.
And, although I never know
Just how much your words mean,
I find it beautiful that
You've touched me in so many places
Without even lifting a finger.
You've touched me in so many places
But I want you to touch me in more.
I want you to hold my face
And touch my cheeks,
Looking into my eyes
As if the world would crumble
If you didn't.
I want you to bury your head in my arms
And plant kisses all over my body.
I want to wear all your hoodies
So the sensation of you
Never has to leave.

And I know that
You've already touched me in so many places,
But my heart won't stop telling me
That it isn't enough.

I Like You
(It's Only Three Words)

I like you.
It's only three little words,
Three gut-wrenching words,
That could destroy everything we have.
But I want to tell you how I feel,
I want to free my thoughts from
The chains they are tied to,
Let them scream
Until their lungs ache with satisfaction,
Let them stop pretending they don't exist
For the amount of time it takes
To choke out those three stupid words.
But then fear floods my head
In never-ending tsunami waves,
What if you don't see forever
In my ugly gray eyes,
What if all the promises you made
Were just sugar-coated lies,
What if I'm left broken with no one
To hear my muffled cries?
This boy could shatter me
And every dream I've ever had

In a matter of seconds
And I know damn well
That I don't want to make myself
Vulnerable like that.
So what are the options?
Keep everything bottled up
While my thoughts consume my world,
Causing me to drown
As the emptiness weighs me down?
Or risk it all
By letting out those three goddamn words,
Which could make everything I've ever
Wanted come true,
Or leave me helpless with no idea of
What the hell to do.
It's just three words
And I'm going to tell you what they are.
The time has come.

What I Said

"I have to tell you something. It's kind of important I guess and
I've been wanting to get it off my chest for a while. So, here goes
nothing. I like you, okay? I'll admit it. And I don't know if you feel
the same way but whenever I talk to you, my day automatically gets
so much better. You can make me happy in a matter of literally half
a second and when I'm with you, I just want to be the best possible
version of myself. You're actually a perfect human being, there's no
other way to describe you, and I know you probably deserve better
than me, but I swear I could appreciate you like no one else could.
You're just so amazing and hilarious and smart and kindhearted
and adorable. How could someone not like you? And it terrifies
me, to finally have someone worth losing. And I just want to move
forward with you and I've been trying so incredibly hard; you have
no idea. I've never put this much time, effort, and thought into
anyone else but you. I'm not entirely sure why, but I guess it has
something to do with you and how you make me want to make the
best of life. You're different from everyone else and my life was so
bland before I met you. I don't think I could ever go back to being
strangers. I really don't. I just want to get to know you even more,
like really know you. I miss when you told me all about how you
have a stupid fear of dogs because your uncle left you in a cage with
a Rottweiler when you were six. I miss when you told me about
how you don't have a favorite color because you don't waste your

time on decisions like that but you do like the way black looks on you. I want to learn more about you and become fascinated with every new detail. I care about you so much. More than you could ever know. And I didn't know what else to do. I just don't know if you're thinking any of this about me and it's driving me insane. And I need to know. You're always in my heart but I just want you in my arms. I don't usually do things like this but, with you, I wanted to give it a try. You're the best thing that's ever happened to me. I'm sorry, but I like you. I hope you can begin to understand that."

Oh my god.

I did not mean to

Tell you all of that,

But the emotions would not stop

Leaping out from the core

Of my heart.

And so that's what I said.

Every feeling I've ever had toward you

Finally put into words.

My Secret

You were my own little secret.
I locked up all the conversations we've ever had,
Clutching them close to my thumping heart.
All of the imaginary strolls along the beach
And nights spent with each other
Took over my optimistic mind.
And soon enough, I couldn't bear to
Hold in the tsunami waves of emotions any longer.
They demolished the lock and fled
Straight for you, but I was terrified
That you wouldn't want them
As much as they needed you.
Not only had I lost my secret,
But fuck, I might also lose you.

The Best Day of My Life

After running my mouth
For God knows how long,
Staring into your
Beautiful eyes
The entire time,
I finally take a moment
To catch my breath.
You don't say a word.
Instead,
You lean in,
Move a lock of hair
Away from my face,
Holding onto it
As your sweet aroma
Fills the air,
And you kiss me.
Your lips taste like
Every fantasy
I've ever created
And the euphoria
Overwhelms me.
When we separate,
We smile so wide

That I'm sure
The whole world
Felt a rush
For the rest of the day.
For the rest of
The best day of my life.

Who Knew Fireworks Could Be So Bright?

Who knew fireworks could be so bright?
When I'm around you, my entire world
Seems as if it's expanding
Because there's just not enough space
To fit all this love into.
A sea of vermillion bleeding into
Royal purple and pink
Surrounds me as we exchange
Words, secrets, and promises.
All the hues around me explode
Because, when true bliss is finally found,
The universe has to let us know.
My signal just happened to be
A magical display of fireworks.

A Messy Kind of Perfect

I know that
What we have
Isn't perfect.
It's more of a
Messy kind of perfect
But I wouldn't want it
Any other way.

Swing Sets & Starry Skies

On one of our first dates,
You took my hand
With limitless possibilities in your palms
And we went to a playground at midnight.
The stars shone from light-years away
But seemed to be smiling at our
Euphoric innocence
All the way from their place
In the sky.
I hopped on a swing set,
My hands loosely grasping
The rusty handles,
As you pushed me to heights
I didn't think I could
Ever reach.
We laughed until our
Cheeks were too sore to speak
So we just sat there in silence,
Your head on my shoulder
Until three in the morning.
It was probably
The happiest I'd ever been
And I prayed that the moment

Would never end.
But, even when it did,
I wasn't disappointed
Because with you,
I knew we'd come back again.
With you,
My starry smiles
Would never leave.

Blue

I remember the day when you told me I
reminded you of the color blue.
At first, I just laughed it off and told you to stop being so deep.
But now I think I know what you meant.
Blue is a color with no limits, like a river
Flowing through an entire city,
Filling it with something beautiful and real.
Like rain pouring down from cotton candy clouds,
Promising a rainbow afterward.
Like the sky hanging above the whole world,
And, even when we're millions of miles away,
We'll both see the same sky when we look up.
This is what our love is like.
Infinite and breathtaking but, most of all,
A brilliant shade of blue.

If We Never Met

If we never met,
I don't think
My world would be the same.
If we never met,
I wouldn't believe in
Shooting stars and dandelion wishes,
I wouldn't always fall asleep
To fantasies of me and you,
I wouldn't write every single poem
About love,
I wouldn't know how captivating
Blue eyes could be,
I wouldn't realize that
Euphoria could feel electromagnetic
As it rushes through my soul,
But most of all,
If we never met,
I would have no idea
What it feels like
To love someone with
Every fiber of my heart
And maybe even more than that.

A Love Too Good to Hide

You took me outside
With sparkles in your eyes
And longing on your lips.
You ran your fingers
Through my frizzy hair,
The sunshine kissing
Our faces,
The clouds embracing
Our shadows.
You traced the lines
On my palms,
Carving each intricate design,
Memorizing each stroke.
You promised that one day
We could always be together.
We wouldn't have to
Sneak into backyards
With the winter wind
Slapping our tinted faces.
We wouldn't have to
Keep our love in
Sealed glass jars.

We wouldn't have to
Count the seconds
Before infinity ended
And our hearts gave out.
Your words were
So pure and gentle.
Just like your eyes,
Staring into mine
As if the world would break
If they didn't.
You pressed your
Hands onto my skin
And I rested my head
On your shoulder,
Until we knew
It was time to run.
All the magic
In the air died
And filled the atmosphere
With a smog of
Destroyed dreams
And chipped memories.
I prayed it wouldn't
Always be like this,
And that someday
We wouldn't have to hide
A love that made
The rest of the universe
Insignificant.

Insane

As much as I love you,
You drive me absolutely insane
And I really hope you know that.

The Stars of Our Hearts

Ever since we decided
To stop keeping our love a secret,
The stars of our hearts
Have seemed to perfectly align
And I'm hoping that
We can lie on our backs,
Hands interlocked,
And stargaze until
Our very last breaths.

My Best Poetry

I just want you to know that
I've written my best poetry
Since falling in love with you.

I Can't Remember

I can't remember what it felt like
To not be in love with you.
I can't remember an absence of radiance
In your big blue eyes.
I can't remember looking at you
And not feeling every emotion in the universe
Race through my fingertips.
I can't remember falling asleep
To the thought of nothingness instead of
Vivid visions of the two of us.
I can't remember a monotonous feeling
In my chest instead of the
Pure elation you engraved into my heart.
I can't remember what it felt like
To not be in love with you,
And to be honest, I don't think
I'd ever want to.

The Five Most Dangerous Words I've Ever Heard

1. Bliss
2. Hope
3. Sorry
4. Promise
5. Love

Alyssa Simone

The Five Most Beautiful Words I've Ever Heard

1. Bliss
2. Hope
3. Sorry
4. Promise
5. Love

Just A Few Months Ago

Just a few months ago,
We were complete strangers,
But now I can't even remember
What it felt like
To not have you in my life.

You

It's you.
You're the one
I want to spend
The rest of my life with.
It's you.
It has always been you.
And I promise
It will always be you.

Without You

When you're not around,
There's a void in my chest
That I can't seem to fill.
I endlessly repeat
In my head
A random conversation we've had,
The melody of your voice
Making my heart burn.
Without you,
Nothing makes sense.
Without you,
I hate the person I am.
I don't know how
I'd ever be able to make it
Without you.

Sunset Soliloquies

You take me to the parking lot
To watch the sunset
Because you remember I once told you
That sunsets are the most beautiful thing in the world to me.
But sitting next to you, I'm not so sure.
I turn my head from you,
To the watercolor sky,
Back to you again,
And it's impossible to say
Which one is more beautiful.
You are so perfect
And delicate.
You are all the good in this world
Wrapped up
Into a singular human being.
And even though I have
Such an ethereal display of colors
Right in front of me,
I realize I'd much rather
Look at you.
You are my sunset.

The Chances We Didn't Take

Today,
I come across a quote that says,
"In the end,
We only regret
The chances we didn't take."
It resonates with
Every cell of my body
And I'm left smiling so wide
I'm sure my face will break.
Because I realize how that one chance
Changed my whole life
And how lucky I am
To be in such a happy relationship
With you.
I have no regrets
Because you're finally mine.
And you're the greatest chance
I've ever taken.

The Sound of Your Voice

Why is it
That the sound
Of your voice
Is more addictive
Than the air
We must breathe
To survive?

Always on My Mind

You are always on my mind
And, to be honest,
I would never want it
Any other way.

When You Hold My Hand

When you hold my hand,
Our fingers lacing together perfectly,
Every fear that has ever
Crept under my skin
Seems to evaporate into thin air
And all I can focus on
Is how absolutely flawless we feel,
Because when we're together
I could never worry.
When your hand's in mine,
I know for sure
That you and me—
We're an infinite type of thing.

Why Do You Always Write About Love?

"Why do you always
Write about love?"
They ask me.
A smile forces itself
Onto my lips
As I answer,
"Because it's the
Only thing that
Keeps me alive."

You Are Good, Too

"I've noticed something about you.
You only see the good in the world,
In people,
In basically everything,
Except for yourself."

One More Time

How is it that
I literally can't go
A few hours
Without seeing you
Before my heart
Begins to twinge
In isolation
And moans your name
As if you are
Its only will
To keep on beating.
One more time.

The Best Friend
I've Ever Had

I think back to
A few months ago,
Before I confessed to you,
And how doubt seemed to
Take over my mind in storm clouds
That I knew were capable of
Torrential rain.
I couldn't figure out
If you saw me as a friend
Or just maybe
A little bit more.
Falling in love
With a close friend
Is utterly terrifying.
I didn't want to lose you
And have no one by my side.
In a single heartbeat,
Things could have turned incredibly bad.
But they didn't.
We're taking on the world together
And you're not just my lover,
You're also the best friend I've ever had.

I Promise I Can Be That Someone

You deserve all the good in this world.
All the crooked smiles
And watercolor skies,
All the lo-fi love songs
And crinkly eyes,
All the summer breezes
And the highest of highs,
You deserve someone who'll love you
Until the universe dies.

A Reason to Care

Before I met you,
I was in a bad place.
I didn't really care about anything
And I spent my life in darkness,
Too afraid to create my own light source.
But you changed me
Because you gave me a reason to care.
And sometimes,
On especially gloomy days,
I think about reverting to
My careless nature,
Where it was easier
To make it through unharmed
By the pain of my own expectations.
But, deep down,
I know I don't want to
Because you gave me such a
Good reason to care
And I won't give up on you.
I can't give up on you.
I'll never stop caring
And it's all because of you.

I Love You

I love you,

Forever and always.

I love you when you play basketball in the rain at two in the
morning and when you come inside shivering, dripping in sweat.

I love you when you make me laugh until my cheeks ache
with joy and you sit there smiling so beautifully that it
makes the universe forget how to breathe for a while.

I love you when your lisp comes out and when the wind messes up
your hair a bit and when you accidentally wear your shirt inside out.

I love you when you make my heart skip a beat, or
two, or ten and when you walk into a room and the
butterflies swarm my stomach all over again.

You may not know it,

But I love you,

With every last piece

Of my once-broken heart.

Sappy Piece of Shit

My heart's on fire,
Strapped into a rollercoaster ride,
Or skydiving.
It's just impossible to decide.
But either way,
Your smile makes euphoria rain down.
I look into your
Ocean eyes and feel like I could drown.
I hope this feeling
Never leaves until the day I die,
You're the best thing in
My life and you don't even have to try.
It's adorable,
I love you more than I can admit
And basically,
This poem is a sappy piece of shit.

Forever

You and me—
We've shared so many beautiful moments.
When I replay them in my mind,
One scene seems to melt into the next
And it's all too surreal.
I try to hold on to them—
All their magical beginnings and
Happily-ever-afters—
Until my fingers go numb
And can't grasp on any longer.
Sometimes I wish I could go back
And relive our times together.
But I know I need to accept
That these heartwarming moments
Sadly cannot last forever.

Energy

It's not like
We don't talk anymore.
Since the very first day
You came into my life,
Or rather,
I decided to enter yours,
We haven't gone more than
Five days
Without keeping in touch.
We still exchange sugar-coated words
And ask about each other's days,
But somehow,
The energy is different,
Like we're both holding our breath
Every time we hit the "send" button,
Like we're becoming fatigued
And trying to hide it,
Like everything could fall apart
In a single moment.
It's the scariest thing
When I realize
That it can
And it probably will.

I Refuse

I can feel us drifting apart.
I can feel us texting less.
I can feel the world
Slipping through my hands,
But I refuse
To let go
Just yet.

Alyssa Simone

We Need to Talk

Over the years,
I've gotten pretty good at lying to myself,
Always having hope
In the darkest of times.
But when I get your text,
I can't think of a single lie
To tell my heart,
As I read the four most painful words
To ever exist:
"We need to talk."
I know what's coming,
But I can't even begin to imagine
What a life without you would look like.
This can't be happening.
I whisper to my bedroom walls,
The sound barely coming out
As tears prick my eyes,
"I can't lose you.
I can't lose you yet."

One More Day

The sand trickles through the hourglass,
Heedless of my passionate pleas.
There's one more day
Until the iridescent sky turns to ash.
One more day
Until smiles are no longer painted
Onto draining faces.
One more day
Until shooting stars explode
Before I can even make my wish.
One more day
Until blood leaks out of my pens
Instead of magical moments with you.
One more day
Until the memories evaporate
As if they never even existed
In the first place.
One more day
Until I'll never see your face,
Hear your laugh,
Or feel your skin
Again.

There's one more day
Until I'll have to learn
How to survive
On my own.

What You Said

"Okay, so I don't know how to say this or if it's going to make sense to you, but I know I have to do this, even if it hurts both of us. I think we should break up. I love you, but you're just too perfect for me and I don't want perfect. It makes things too easy. And I don't trust myself with perfect anyway because I somehow fuck up everything in life. And I don't wanna fuck you up. You deserve better than that. You deserve better than me. I just don't think we're the right people for each other. Basically, I should be happy around you, but I'm not, and I think that's a red flag. I don't fully understand it because like I said, you're perfect, so just know that you did nothing wrong and it has everything to do with me and my own issues. I'm really sorry, but I need to end this before I hurt you even more. I hope you find someone who's just as perfect as you. And don't settle for any less, okay?"

I nod and fix my gaze on the floor. "I understand" is all I can manage to choke out.

"Good. *Au revoir* then."

"What?"

"Oh, sorry. *Au revoir*. It means goodbye until we meet again in French. I don't know, I thought it was cool."

"It is." I almost crack a smile. Almost. "*Au revoir*," I say, but by the time the words depart from my lips, you're already out the door, ready to move on to a new chapter in your life that I won't be a part of.

Au revoir.

Nobody Cares About the Broken

Tonight
I am broken.
My stomach is knotted
And I can feel my throat closing up.
I've found out the truth:
I didn't make you happy.
I'm just another girl
With a fragile heart
That I should have known
You would shatter.
I had faith in you,
But I guess I was wrong
Because you never cared,
Not even a little.
I just wish I could have fast-forwarded
To the end,
Where I am not yours
And you are not mine.

I pray that one day
The pain will subside,
But tonight, I am so broken.
And nobody cares
About the broken.

Empty

I never expected heartbreak to feel this way. It's the feeling of carrying around an empty heart, like keeping a dead dog. It's the feeling of forest fires burning through my bones, wondering why I wasn't good enough for you. It's the feeling of a billion poisonous memories rushing through my head, desperate to swallow me whole. It's the feeling of a gray aura surrounding me as all I do is sleep, so I won't have to feel. It's the feeling of holding the weight of the world on my shoulders until it suddenly shatters, the glass shards digging themselves into my fragile skin. It's the feeling of waking up and not remembering until the knife of truth wedges its way into my mind. It's the feeling of eating nothing but an expired pack of colored marshmallows I found in the basement, becoming sicker and sicker with each one I pop into my mouth, but not stopping because it's better than tasting your cold lips on mine. It's the feeling of longing stuck between my teeth and in the bags underneath my bloodshot eyes. It's the feeling of throwing up everything I once had into a public toilet, letting the digested marshmallows and spit fall out of my mouth, because I just can't contain my emotions anymore.

Sometimes, all I can do is scribble a few lines of sad poetry in notebooks full of old love poems, but that's just my way of coping with the pain. That's just my way of pretending I'm feeling fine, even though I know that will never be true. That's just my way of acting as if this pain doesn't exist. Most people say when they feel pain, they feel it everywhere. The sensation races through their bodies and fills them with everything. But I don't feel that way at all. For me, pain is just another void I know I can never fill. And without you, I'm afraid I'll just feel empty forever.

Tough Girls Don't Cry

Tough girls don't cry,
Everyone tells me,
The phrase slipping from their lips
Like molasses.
It drowns my mind
And the lies I have been told.
Because I am a girl.
And I am weak.
How can I keep
The tears from streaming
And staining my hideous face
When bees sting my throat,
When filthy hands
Strangle my heart,
And when the glass sky above me
Is shattering,
Its shards raining down
And slicing my bare skin
With evil words?
Why is it a sin
To have emotions?
I guess that's just
The way it is.

It's the rule that is whispered in the ears
Of all insecure girls.
Tough girls don't cry.
So make sure you run away
Before they can see your face
And don't forget to slam
The door behind you—

Fragile

Every moment with you felt so fragile.
Like I was carrying something so sacred
In my weakened grasp,
And one wrong move,
One slip-up,
Could ruin the best thing I've ever had.
You spent months tiptoeing around the truth,
Around a lack of love that only grew and grew,
Because there was no denying I'd lose you forever
If the secret got out and I ever knew.
Being part of your story was more than enough.
I was so proud of the bond we formed
And how your name always lit up my phone.
You said I helped you through your toughest times
And it was so rewarding to see how you'd grown.
I never thought we'd go back to being strangers,
That you'd walk right by me, pretending to forget,
As the humiliation washed over me,
And flooded my thoughts with pure regret.
I tried so hard to hold us together.

I buried my defects deep within my soul,
A burden I was so sure I could handle.
But I wasn't strong enough and it all fell apart.
I guess that's what happens when you let the truth unravel.
I guess that's what happens when your love is fragile.

I Deserved a Better Goodbye

I deserved a better goodbye.
After staying up until four in the morning with you
every night, arguing over which *Star Wars* movie was
the best, I truly thought we had something special.
All the geometry periods spent drawing lopsided
hearts in each other's notebooks, all the days after
school when you bought me bubble tea, all the days
I stayed at your house to "work on a project";
Those were the best days of my life.
You patched a piece of my heart that I
Thought I would never get back,
And yet,
You're already in another girl's arms.
All the text messages and goofy conversations stopped,
And you could barely even tell me why,
And I swear to you, I deserved a better goodbye.

I ~~Hate~~ Love You

I hate you.
And I lie when I say
We shared beautiful times together.
It wasn't real.
Don't try to convince me that
I love you.
(now read from bottom to top)

Too Perfect

Some things in life
Just seem too perfect
And that scares us,
So we let them go
And break them
Before they have
A chance
To break us.

Sweet Lies

Sugary smiles.
Candy-coated I-love-you's.
The sweetest of lies.

For Just a Moment

For just a moment,
You seemed within reach,
So I put out my hand,
But all I could feel
Was the bitterness
Of the empty air.

Sleepless Nights

I roll over for what must be
The hundredth time
In my bed.
I flip my heated pillow
And rest my head on it.
The pillow I have soaked with tears.
The pillow of lies and broken promises.
The pillow that whispers to me throughout the night,
Daring me to fall asleep,
Knowing I will fail.
I rearrange my covers.
Blanket on: too hot.
Blanket off: shivering with the frigid air.
Or maybe I'm shivering with fear.
Fear of the unknown,
Fear of the future,
Fear of never forgetting about you.
You haunt me into the early hours of the day,
Reminding me that I was too weak,
Reminding me that you will never come back,
But flashing your face before my eyes
In order to break me down.

I fumble for the stuffed bear
You gave me so long ago,
Back when I was important to you.
I clutch it toward my heart.
My heart, which is now shattered,
The pieces never cleaned up.
My heart, which you stole from me
And claimed as your own.
I look outside my window
Just in time to see dawn break.
The radiance of pastel pinks
Seeping into neon oranges
Creating a display for me.
Finally, the sun peeks out,
Consoling me,
Telling me to get some sleep,
Assuring me that everything will be okay.
I smile and listen to her words,
Her words of warmth,
Not like your empty words
That held no meaning,
But were spewed out to cause me pain.
At last, sleep escorts me
Into its bittersweet world.
It takes over my mind,
Flooding it with memories.
The memories of who you used to be
Before the world came crashing down on us,
And you left me behind.

When I believe this might be
The first time in forever
That I actually fall asleep,
Your face comes back
And taunts me.
My alarm goes off.
I sit up and rub my eyes.
Yet another sleepless night.

Why I Can't Write About You Anymore

I don't know why,
But I just can't
Write poetry about you
Anymore.
I guess some things
Just hurt too much.

I Miss You

I miss you.
So incredibly much.
My heart feels empty,
Numb,
Lost,
Without you by my side
To help it keep beating.
It's only been a few days
Since I've heard your
Delicate voice
And looked into your
Captivating eyes,
But it feels like forever
And I don't know
How much longer
I can go.
I just want to hold you
And never let go,
To feel you in my hands
And sense the sparks
All over again,
To kiss you
Until our lungs burn

While still being left
Unsatisfied.
But for now,
I miss you.
So incredibly much.
And I can't help but wonder
If deep down,
Maybe you're missing me
A little bit, too.

He Doesn't Want You

He doesn't want you.
The realization finally settles in,
Forming a tornado in the pit of my stomach
And causing a torrential downpour
Over the rest of my world.
I was naive.
Why would someone as incredible as you
Ever stay with a girl like me?
A girl who feels a bit too sad all the time,
A girl whose insecurities dictate her life,
A girl who says things without thinking sometimes,
A girl who is mediocre at just about everything,
A girl who doesn't do too well on her physics tests,
Even though she studies for hours.
A girl who stays up until midnight and wonders why
She can barely open her eyes in the morning.
A girl who wishes she could be anyone
But herself.
Maybe if I was her, you would want me.
Maybe then, I could finally be happy.
Maybe then, my heart could be pieced back together.
Maybe then, I wouldn't think about what it would feel like
To die every time I see your face.

Maybe then, I'd actually believe in myself a little bit,
But that's a pretty hard thing to do
When it's clear that
No one will ever want me.

Nostalgia

When Nostalgia comes darting back
From the place in my heart
Where I thought I left her,
She begins to pant,
Sweat beads sliding down
Her porcelain skin.
She presses her lips
To my ear,
Letting silky words unravel and
Form cobwebs of
The things that used to be
A part of my life.
She sews quilts of memories
Before my eyes,
Of beaches at midnight
With a violet sky
Looking down from above,
Of a couple sitting
With their fingers intertwined,
The winter wind
Bringing them together,
Of climbing to the tops
Of sycamore trees

Before their branches grow frail
And send life falling
To the brittle ground.
Nostalgia brings these scenes
Back to me.
They flood my mind in
Waves that I was sure
Had receded.
She whispers,
"You can't escape the past,"
The sugar-coated phrase
Causing all my hopes to decay.
"So don't even try to run."

Alyssa Simone

I Remember a Time

I remember a time
When exuberance paraded through life.
I remember a time when the sun's sanguine rays
Peered through my window and darted for our eyes,
A time when your dainty fingers meticulously braided
Strands of my boring black hair,
A time when our tiny bare feet slapped the wet grass
To keep up with the chorus of the ice cream truck,
A time when I painted streaks of lavender
Onto your grimy, chipped fingernails,
A time when we knotted the stems of
Glistening, white daisies into flower crowns.
A time when we ate a whole container of frosting
And it stained our tongues a brilliant seafoam green.
I remember a time when the billions of colors
That gushed through every part of my universe
Hadn't yet faded into nothingness
And turned into black and white.

If You Were Here

I look out the window.

Wow.

Life truly is beautiful.

But there's no denying that

It would be so much

More beautiful

If you were here, too.

The Colors of Us

Red is for the rage I felt when you left,
Orange is for the radiance of our bereft.
Yellow is for the days we made each other laugh,
Green is for the envy when I see her in your lap.
Blue is for the sadness of not having you next to me,
Purple is for the hope I had when tears were all I could see.
Pink is for the trust we had, never to be broken,
Gray is for your aura, which only left me heartbroken.
Black is for a stab in the back with the sharpest of knives.
White is for the memories we'll have for the rest of our lives.
And I know I say that everything is fine,
But right now, to tell the truth, I feel color-blind.

I Remember the Person You Used to Be

I remember the person you used to be,
I remember last June when we climbed to the top of the sycamore
tree in my backyard and your voice in my ear sounded like the
wind singing a lullaby to a child. The orange sun was sinking
into the watercolor sky; everything about that moment was
perfect. You ran your fingers through my hair as I stared into
your soothing eyes. You told me that I meant the world to you
and, at that moment, fireworks exploded from my heart, their
hues bursting in infinite directions. Your words tasted like
candy and I let their flavor—I think it was watermelon, no,
strawberry—melt onto my tongue. I swayed my head to the
rhythmic beating of our hearts and you wrapped your arms around
me. It was on that day that I handed you my heart, daintily
wrapped in magenta paper, and I trusted you to treasure it. The
night smiled at us, smiled wide and showcased all of its teeth.
And now, three months later, love has become a foggy memory
because, as soon as I gave you my heart, you ran away without
even looking back to make sure I hadn't fallen out of our tree.

Running Back

As much as I hate to admit it,
If you came running back to me,
Begging on your knees
For forgiveness,
I would take you back
With open arms,
Despite all the scars
You left me with.

Remember?

Remember?
Remember when life was good and the world tasted like sunshine?
I know it seems like a while ago but I
Promise that there was a time when
Laughter bounced off your bedroom walls
And echoed through your soul.
You weren't afraid to kiss in the dark or
Show me your messy, 8 am hair,
Or open up about the parts of yourself that needed healing.
Remember?
I know this part always becomes a bit
Blurry, but one day you told me
How I just didn't make you feel the same anymore and how
You needed someone who wasn't as perfectly mundane as me.
Remember?
I think we both cried a lot and skipped school the next day because
We couldn't handle the thought of walking right past each other
As if we didn't spend the last six months of our lives together.
As if we were strangers.
Remember?
This is the part that's a bit dark even though
Dawn was breaking around us
But you told me that you'd made your decision and there was

Nothing I could do to change your mind.

After that night, my smiles disappeared before they could even form

While you seemed happier on your own than you ever were

When we were together.

Remember?

I felt like I had lost the person who meant the most to me

But I guess this is just the way life unfolds sometimes.

It crumbles the moment it touches your fingertips

And there's no way to stop it.

I guess this is what happens when you put every ounce of trust

You've ever had

Into your first love, if you even call me that.

I don't think you answered any of my phone calls the next day

So I just read through our old conversations and

Looked through old pictures from when everything felt okay

And I finally realized you were gone.

And I guess you can't remember anything after this.

Her

It hasn't even been a month
And you've already found someone new.
She's everything I could never be.
You tell everyone how
She smells of rose water
And tastes like strawberries and sugar,
How her laughter sounds like
A reincarnation of innocence,
And her voice like
The melody from your favorite song.
And I know I shouldn't be watching,
But I can tell you like her better.
I know you kiss her longer
And you hug her a little tighter.
I know you call her later
And you say your I-love-you's louder.
I know you're trying harder
And your love for her is deeper.
I can see it in your eyes.
You feel something toward her
That you never felt toward me.
You feel alive as she
Pours the poetry into your soul

The way I never could.
I hate her,
But I wish I was her.
You love her
But I'll never be her.

Jealousy

When Jealousy crawls beneath my skin
And causes my veins to vibrate with rage,
I cannot help but let the tyrant
Overtake me.
It dives into my body,
Wrenching my ribs,
Bashing my bones,
And harassing my heart.
It torments my mind and tackles it
With thoughts of
"I wish, I wish, I wish."
It paints my face green
And pulls my eyes open
When all I want to do
Is look away forever.
It forms a volcano that erupts
From the pit of my stomach
And sends molten lava spilling
From my fingertips,

Scorching my scarred hopes
Until they shatter into shards
That silently slice my soul.
It feasts off of my wounded flesh,
Devouring my self-esteem
Until it becomes nothing
But a faded memory,
Crumpling it up
Like a confiscated note,
And burying it below the earth
Like the corpse of the one it loved most.
With all I've ever had
Closing in on me
Faster than I can handle,
I give up
And allow Jealousy to swallow me whole.
With that,
Everything becomes nothing
Before I can even understand
Why stars only come out
When we are surrounded by nothing but darkness.

Is It Possible for Colors to Drain?

Is it possible for colors to drain?
Because when we used to get lost together,
Sitting on my rooftop,
The overpowering hues of the sunset
Seemed to take us with them.
Fuchsia would dissolve into lavender,
Which would bleed into a fiery orange,
All the colors creating a beautiful work of art.
Our souls would drift off with the paint streaks,
Swirling inward and becoming one with the sky.
And then it all seemed to burst,
Different shades exploding this way and that.
Our hearts shattered our glass chests
Just so they could soar into the canvas
And ensure that we would remember this time
Forever.
But now, everything has changed.
Only your shadow remains
Next to me,
A hollow space with no purpose,
Mocking my solitude.
I thought the pain of losing you

Would be bearable,
But I've had to suffer by watching the world
Slowly come to an end.
My murky gray eyes
Stare at what lies before me
And become weaker with every passing second.
The entire scene is lightly sketched
With a dull-tipped pencil,
Filled in with feeble strokes of nothing.
All the dead reds and fading oranges
Diminish before my eyes,
And so
I send the remains of my spirit with them.
It spirals toward the clutter
And I watch it plummet downward,
Along with the colors that
Couldn't ever have been bright.
Time seems to forget its function
And all I can do is stare
As whatever is left of life comes crashing,
And worse than a cacophony,
All that follows is silence,
Which I never would have imagined
Could be so loud.
The colors are gone
And I question their existence in the first place.
I have my answer.
Yes, my old friend, it is possible for colors to drain
And if I could have drained on that night too,

Trust me, I wouldn't hesitate,
Even if it meant I could have you back.
You don't drink poison
Unless you want to die
And I'd rather spend the rest of eternity
Draining with what I used to call
Colors.

The Way I Loved You

There was something so special about the way I loved you.
There was something so special about the way
You could put my
Disheveled head and restless heart
At complete ease
And that's saying a lot, coming from
An over-worrier, over-thinker, and over-lover.
There was something about your eyes
That twinkled like the stars
On the loneliest of nights,
And the way your slurred words,
Your raspy voice that was hungry for sleep,
Were enough to keep either of us
From hanging up the phone before six o'clock in the morning.
There was something so absolutely astonishing
About the way you let your emotions
Pour from your heart like acrylic paint,
All the joyous yellows juxtaposed with dejected blues
Coming together to create a masterpiece
That belonged in a museum,
And I was lucky enough to get the first glimpse.
There was something so addicting about
Sacrificing every piece of my soul

For someone who refused to even
Break off a sliver for me in return.
I romanticized an unrequited love,
Tried so desperately to convince myself
That you were gazing into my lost, terrified eyes
And witnessing an entire galaxy of everlasting beauty.
But, deep down in my core, I knew that
You'd never put me on the same pedestal
That I constructed for you
Or fantasize about the impossible
Just because, if only for a moment,
It helped me forget that every single time you
Made my heart flutter, it didn't mean anything anymore.
You always did say idealism was nothing more
Than a soul-crushing destiny after all
And, no matter how badly I wish it weren't true,
I need to stop making excuses
And so I scream with everything I have left in me
Until my vocal cords ache with honesty.
There was something so draining about the way I loved you.
Because it's now crystal clear to me that
There was nothing I could ever say or do
To make me more than just some girl to you.
There was nothing so special about the way I loved you.

Fading Away

Bittersweet remnants
Of times we spent together
Now fading away.

Sometimes

Sometimes, the memories swallow me whole.
Sometimes, I feel wounded before the shots are even fired.
Sometimes, the blood seeps out before I even sense the pain.
Sometimes, I start drowning before I even touch the water.
Sometimes, I choke before I even open my mouth.
Sometimes, I cry before I even know what's wrong.
Sometimes, I run away before I even say goodbye.
Sometimes, the memories swallow me whole,
But they always leave me feeling empty inside,
Which is just another reason why
I'm never going to try to remember again.

Your Eyes

Your eyes are the bullets that you fire at me
Just so you can watch me cower in fear
While your ego frolics
Through a field of once-golden daisies
Whose hues have now faded into nothingness.
Your eyes drain me
Of all the strength I once possessed
And force me to shrivel up
Like a dying flower,
Gasping for breath.
Your rich blue eyes
Are like an endless sky
Until the black holes begin to come into view
And the beauty suddenly disappears.
Your eyes are the twinkling stars
Speckled against the night-sky canvas
Because, although they shine at first,
They'll always vanish and leave me wondering why.
Your eyes are like the chipped white paint on my walls,
The reflection of deception on a window,
A half-finished poem I scribbled in pencil,
An old candy wrapper that crinkles with a single touch,
And a shattered glass doll,

The pieces never picked up.
Your eyes distracted me
Every time you told a lie,
Every time you broke a promise,
And every time you said I love you
When you no longer meant it.
Your eyes are venomous
And have haunted me
In all the nightmares I've had since you've left.
I can draw your ghostly eyes from memory,
And if I ever do
I'll immediately tear them up,
But, before they're gone forever,
I'll be sure to color them in gray.

Cut My Hair

Back when we were together,
You always told me to never cut my hair.
But deep down,
I've always wanted to.
I used to be afraid
That you wouldn't love me anymore
So I kept it long
Just so I could gain your approval.
But now that you're out of my life,
You no longer get to dictate
If I keep my hair long
Or short
Or curly
Or straight
Or black
Or fucking bright red.
I grab a pair of scissors
And just start cutting,
Cutting away all the spots
Where your hands got tangled,
All the spots
You have poisoned with your touch.
I look in the mirror

And at the six inches of hair
Decorating the floor beneath me.
And for the first time
Since the day it all fell apart,
I finally catch myself
Smiling.

And Yet I Smile

I expect the sun to beam in the sky,
But it remains dark, filled with fear,
And yet I smile.
I walk down the halls all alone,
My only comfort
The music blasting from my earbuds,
And yet I smile.
I suffer through an endless cycle
Of getting my hopes up too high
And having them crash down on my feeble figure,
And yet I smile.
The words that I've always wanted to say
Get stuck in my throat before I can squeak them out,
And yet I smile.
I was so sure that you were mine,
And then you turned around and decided
She was better than me,
And yet I smile.
All good things must come to an end,
And when everything I've ever wanted out of life
Ends with it,
You'd expect me to lose my strength.
But if you just look over,

It's clear that despite the emptiness
I feel in my stomach,
My soul isn't broken just yet.
A tear of survival slides down my cheek.
And yet I smile.

Alyssa Simone

My Heart Bleeds to Remind Me I'm Alive

Although I have been healing,
There are times when
My heart begins to bleed out
From all the wounds you left it with.
But, despite all the pain,
It never stops
Beating,
It never stops
Pumping life through my body.
The pain is just another reminder
That I haven't gone completely numb,
That I'm still making it by,
Day by day.
So bleed!
Bleed until my heart is soaked
In crimson,
Bleed!
Bleed until it doesn't hurt me
Anymore.

Bleed!
I'll be okay.
My heart bleeds
To remind me I'm alive.

You Don't Feel Like Home Anymore

I think the reason
It took me so long to stop thinking about you
Was the feeling of comfort you emanated.
You were my home.
And I was so used to
Returning to you
Every single day.
But now, you don't bring me
Consolation.
You make me feel like
A stranger in my own skin,
So weak and fragile,
And I'm tired of feeling like
Anything but the most
Powerful woman I know.
I don't need you,
And you don't feel like home anymore.

I Tried to Fix You

As we grew closer,
I started to discover your flaws,
But I loved you in spite of them all
And tried to help you overcome them.
That was my first mistake.
You shouldn't love someone
Because of who you think they'll become
When they're around you.
You should love someone
Who admits that they're imperfect,
And works on bettering themselves for you
With every passing day.
But I took matters into my own hands,
And tried to perfect you
Even though it was clear
You didn't want to change.
You were broken,
And I tried to fix you.

Bad Poetry

I really wish I could do something more than write bad poetry.
I envy those who can grip pens—
Ideas spilling out of them onto snowy white pages,
Filling them with inky words,
Although they always seem to be the right words,
But me—
I can never describe the thoughts that live in my mind
In simple strings of letters one would find in a dictionary.
I run my fingers against the book,
Hoping it will save me.
But if I could write lines with power—
And trust me, I've tried—
What would it mean coming from a teenage girl
Who only pollutes the world?
Whenever the emotions that hide within
The deepest chambers of my heart
Become too strong to choke back down,
I just keep writing and writing so I won't have to feel,
Until there's nothing left to say,
And this is why, when it's two in the morning,
Instead of getting the sleep that I so desperately need,
I'm sitting on my rooftop and filling every notebook I own with
The words that don't know how to keep themselves locked up.

The longing to fill nothingness with everything overtakes me,
And pretty soon,
I'm scribbling words into the margins of math
Notes with a dull-tipped pencil
I found on the floor,
Not even knowing how I'm putting them
Together, but at the same time,
Refusing to stop.
I don't really know what I'm trying to say,
But then again, I need to say something,
And if the only way I can do that is through writing bad poetry,
Then I will not stop until every little voice
Screaming within my veins
Knows that what they have to say makes the universe
Shine a little bit brighter every night.

Your Name

When my eyes take a stroll through this colorless world,
With evergreen forests of emotion being chopped down to nothing,
They always land on the lopsided letters of your nostalgic name.
They're scribbled into the margins of last year's science notes,
Etched into the sycamore tree that towers over my backyard,
Written in invisible ink every time our paths cross,
Sliced into the air with its six letters shrieking,
Listed in my contacts with hearts still parading behind it,
Drawn into foggy mirrors after every silent shower I take,
But above all, they're engraved into my heavy heart,
Thumping in my ears like the shouting of a sacred secret.
And even though each sickening syllable
Causes the clusters of colors to drain from this world,
I cannot stop the sound from escaping my lips.
But the truth is, your name spells out poison and decay,
So, whenever it enters the atmosphere,
It only pollutes the sapphire sky
Until it, too, becomes the color of your name—
Gray.

My Favorite Lie

My favorite lie
You ever told me was
I love you.
We all know that love
Isn't about carving initials
Into each other's hearts
And then running away
With the blood-stained knife,
The crooked letters serving
As my only reminder of
A time when you were
A part of my life.
We all know that love
Isn't about waking up
To the feel of congealed tears
Against blotchy cheeks
And cowering in fear
When faced with reality.
We all know that love
Isn't about testing who
Has the highest pain tolerance
When the bullets are fired
At the mind and mistaken

Alyssa Simone

For shots of undying love.
Love isn't supposed to
Feel like a sin,
So why is it
That, every time I think of you,
I feel obliged to drop
To my knees and pray
For God's forgiveness?
Why is it that I can't
Even look at myself
In the mirror without
Feeling the glass digging
Its way into my already wounded skin?
Why is it that
I'm still reminiscing
About every last hug,
Every last kiss,
And every last I love you?
Love—
It wasn't love.
It wasn't bliss.
It wasn't my happily-ever-after.
This is only once upon a time
Because one day I'll find myself a love
That makes all the pain I've had to endure
From losing you,
Feel worth it.

Where It All Went Wrong

The more that I
Started to like you,
The less that I
Started to like myself,
And I think that's where
It all went wrong.

Memories No More

I won't think of you.
You're a hushed melody of
Memories no more.

Can You Hear My Heartbeat?

Can you hear my heartbeat?
Can you hear the steady thump,
Even after all it has been through?
It continues to bring me life,
Although its surface is cracked.
This makes the heart
A more powerful force
Than the countless memories
You have engraved into my bones.
If you ever decide to come back,
Please don't bring up
Our past.
Instead, just answer my simple question:
Can you hear my heartbeat?

Over You

I'm over you.
You no longer bring brilliant colors to my world,
Nor do you pervade my every thought.
You no longer unintentionally make me smile,
Nor do you cause my heart to pound.
You don't make me feel good about myself.
You're just another reminder of
Broken promises and deception.
I don't need that in my life anymore.
And now, here I am,
Truthfully able to say that
I'm over you.

Only One of Us Was Hurting

I always get questions about
How I was able to heal so quickly,
How I was able to move on from someone
Who made me the happiest
I ever was.
(What they don't know
Is that you suffocated my heart
And also made me the saddest
I ever was.)
But my response is that,
After you left me,
Only one of us was hurting,
And that made me the weakest
I ever was.
(But I've become the strongest,
Most powerful
I ever was
Ever since
I've refused to continue
Hurting alone.)

The Idea of a Love

I don't miss you,
But I miss the idea of a love
That makes me feel infinite.
I miss the idea of a love
Where you take time out of your busy schedule
Just to hear them talk about their day.
I miss the idea of a love
Where you wake up an hour early
Just to make them their favorite breakfast
And a cup of coffee in the morning,
Despite how your body is practically begging
For more sleep.
I miss the idea of a love
Where you'd drop everything in an instant
Just to be by their side,
Supporting them in their darkest moments,
Hoping your hugs will heal them.
But lucky for me,
There's always self-love,
And tomorrow morning
I'm waking up an hour early
Just to treat myself to my favorite breakfast
And a cup of coffee,

Because right now,
I am overflowing with love,
And I think the perfect person
To give all of it to right now
Would have to be
Myself.

Alyssa Simone

Truthfully Okay

When my friends ask me how I am,
I tell them I think I'm okay,
But more importantly,
For the first time in months,
I'm not telling them a lie.

I'm Happy You're Happy

She makes you glow
In a way I never could.
But one day I'll make someone
Outshine every galaxy in this world,
And for now,
I'm happy you're happy.

Alyssa Simone

A Love Letter to Myself

I love myself and, even if that's not true, I'll
keep saying it until I believe it.

Of course, I love the features that compose who I am, like my
kindness, my bravery, my ability to write as if my life depends on it.
But it's the little things about myself, the tiny little surprises hidden
in the folds of my heart, that I think I love the most. I love the way
my face brightens when I talk about one of my passions. I love the
way my hair falls in front of my face when I'm working super hard
in class or trying to finish a test before the bell rings. I love the way
I smile, how the corners of my mouth seem to melt as they turn
upwards. I love the way my eyes get all wrinkly when I'm happy, my
brown eyes that seem to contain all the secrets in the universe. I love
the way I'm so polite to everyone, even strangers who know nothing
about my story. I love the way my fingers turn red after I finish
playing a song on the ukulele, the way I can't help but stutter when
I order my grande iced caramel macchiato from Starbucks, the
way my voice echoes across the room whenever I really want to be
heard, the way my hair gets carried away with the wind on winter
afternoons, the way time stops when I enter a room. I love the way
I write because it's my favorite thing to do, and each letter, each
stroke, is so unbelievably real and raw. I love the way I write poems
when I'm stressed out and how my cheeks turn pink when someone
asks if they can read one. I love the way the most insignificant

things, like a stray cat in the street or a rainbow after it downpours,
can fascinate me. I love the way I never sacrifice who I am just to
please other people. I love how all my quirks make me unique,
and how they all come together to create the person I am today.
I love myself, and if I'm being honest, I'm starting to
believe those words more and more each day.

Lost and Found

I think I was so focused
On giving you all the love
In my soul,
That I lost myself
Along the way.
I was okay with being unhappy,
As long as you were smiling.
I didn't know who I was anymore
And, when you left me,
I thought I never would again.
But eventually
I was able to fall in love again,
But this time,
It was with myself.
I started putting my own needs first
Because you can't love another person
Until you learn to love yourself.
And slowly
I collected all the pieces of myself
I thought were gone forever.
I was lost with you,
But now you are gone,
And I have been found.

A List of Love

The other day,
I asked a friend to name
All the things she loved.
She began listing and listing,
Naming everything from
Her best friends,
To dogs,
To ice cream cake
And dandelions.
Eventually, I interrupted
And asked how long it would take
Before she named herself.
It is not selfish
To love yourself.
And, if you're reading this,
I want you to take out a pen
And a piece of paper
And list all the things you love.
And make sure
You're at the top of that list.

I Wanna Use My Voice

I wanna use my voice!
I wanna hear it echoing through
Every single soul;
I wanna make my thoughts whole
Because all of these half-finished poems
Are making me lose what's left of my mind.
I wanna use my voice
Because I've already heard thousands
Of other people use theirs
And there will never be a melody as sweet
As the one that comes from my core.
I'm tired of countering every
"Hey, what's on your mind?"
With "Oh nothing, I'm doing just fine"
Because my world is overflowing with words
That I'm afraid will slip through my fingertips
If I seal my lips
For just another moment longer.
This girl is filled with
Bright thoughts,
Midnight thoughts,
I'm-happiest-when-I-write thoughts.
Hurried thoughts,
Scurried thoughts,

Why-do-I-feel-so-worried thoughts?
Aching thoughts,
Flaking thoughts,
This-is-a-chance-I'm-taking thoughts.
I've had enough of counting all the places
Where no one will look for me,
Pretending I had hope
When tears were all I could see,
Wondering if everyone who looks at my face
In the hallways thinks, "Who is she?"
The gears in my brain started to turn
Just like I did from all the opportunities
That welcomed me with open arms.
I will never again forget the sound of my own voice,
I will never again forget what freedom tastes like,
I will never again use insecurities to fill the cracks between my bones
Because this
Is the moment I've been waiting for my entire life.
This is the moment where I make myself vulnerable
By giving everything I have,
But maybe that's not such a bad thing because
I believe everyone who reads these words
Will be able to find their voices,
Just like I did.
And after all that wasted time
Spent bottling up my fears,
Here I am,
Stating loud and clear that
I'm gonna use my voice!

Au Revoir (Goodbye Until We Meet Again)

Au revoir, you whispered,
The phrase lingering in the heavy summer air.
Would we really meet again?
I watched as you kissed the setting sun,
Sent your soul up to the violet sky,
And let your words spill through your fingers.
My world remained silent,
And it seemed to be shrinking.
Tree branches swayed with the breeze
And you slowly walked away,
Taking with you a lifetime of memories
I wrapped into your skin.
I would never see your smiles again,
The really big ones that almost fell off your face.
I wouldn't see your seafoam eyes
That seemed to laugh whenever
We were together.
They spoke in poetic sentences
When your mouth was too scared to,
And saved me from drowning in my own body.
I stared and stared until all I
Could see was darkness,

In a place that seemed much too big for me
To conquer alone.
And healing the damage you caused
Was not easy,
But it wasn't impossible either.
I pretend I am seeing myself through your eyes,
Watching a no longer broken girl frantically
Writing away her wounds
In a worn notebook with dog-eared pages,
Her jet black hair hiding her thoughts.
She can only breathe words
And she relies on her pen to carry them
Out of her heart.
She's thinking back to that day you left,
When the universe tasted sour,
And she beams with pride about how far she's come.
But no matter how many times she
Tries to replay the moment,
The only words she can remember are
Au revoir.
(This is officially goodbye.
But I hope one day when we're
Older,
Wiser,
And you've read through these pages
A couple hundred times,
We can meet again.)

CPSIA information can be obtained
at www.ICGtesting.com
Printed in the USA
LVHW030832170821
695469LV00009B/1147

9 781954 095373